Shine On

CORINNE KING

Shine On © Copyright 2024 Corinne King

All rights reserved. No part of this publication may be reproduced, distributed or transmitted in any form or by any means, including photocopying, recording, or other electronic or mechanical methods, without the prior written permission of the publisher, except in the case of brief quotations embodied in critical reviews and certain other noncommercial uses permitted by copyright law.

Although the author and publisher have made every effort to ensure that the information in this book was correct at press time, the author and publisher do not assume and hereby disclaim any liability to any party for any loss, damage, or disruption caused by errors or omissions, whether such errors or omissions result from negligence, accident, or any other cause.

Adherence to all applicable laws and regulations, including international, federal, state and local governing professional licensing, business practices, advertising, and all other aspects of doing business in the US, Canada or any other jurisdiction is the sole responsibility of the reader and consumer.

Neither the author nor the publisher assumes any responsibility or liability whatsoever on behalf of the consumer or reader of this material. Any perceived slight of any individual or organization is purely unintentional.

The resources in this book are provided for informational purposes only and should not be used to replace the specialized training and professional judgment of a health care or mental health care professional.

Neither the author nor the publisher can be held responsible for the use of the information provided within this book. Please always consult a trained professional before making any decision regarding treatment of yourself or others.

Paperback ISBN: 979-8-89316-277-6

Ebook ISBN: 979-8-89316-278-3

Hardcover ISBN: 979-8-89316-329-2

To my Minden Grace and Mary Lafitte
who I am beyond blessed to watch grow up

To my momma who is
and always will be the woman I adore

To our Gracious Lord in Heaven
for inviting me to share our story to help others

To my husband who knows me
inside and out, just like my momma did

Acknowledgments

For Lynnette-

A sincere thank you from the bottom of my heart for your impact and support as my life coach to help transition myself to become a storyteller. Your gentle spirit and support were invaluable. Keep shining bright dear friend.

Introduction

My *fearfully* and *wonderfully* made daughter's, quiet your hearts and let me tell you a story of God's love. It began with a girl born just outside St. Louis, Missouri. She had a wondrous childhood running wild with friends and riding buses into the city as a parent free teenager. The year she turned fifteen her father accepted a new job, in a new state. She packed up her room and they moved to the small town of Athens, Texas. She was incredibly relieved to see for herself that not of those country bumpkins riding a horse to school like she had seen in the movies. She followed her heart's calling and became a nurse and married. She found herself in another sleepy town in Texas, Madisonville. Here is where one of her many prayers was answered. She became my mother and turned into one of the most selfless women I have ever known. It's the place where our story together begins, my mother and I. The loss of my mother was the greatest grief I have ever felt. God walked beside me the entire way and redeemed our relationship until the very end. No matter where you are with your relationship with your mother. God will always shine upon your face and give His gift of peace. I wrote this book to honor her legacy and to share the deep love we have for each other.

*"I will praise You because I have been fearfully and wonderfully made.
Your works are wonderful, and I know this very well."*
Psalms 139:14

Corinne King

Saltines

Saltine crackers are still *her*. I can taste the simple and salty from my childhood as we used to share a sleeve of saltines often. She is the salt of my tears when I cry. I find comfort in the salt knowing that I can still feel her. "The salt of the earth" (Matthew 5:13). My mother's essence was of the earth, and she demonstrated how to be that salt. She was a pure, honest, and humble person who loved the Lord with all her heart. She exemplified James 4:10, "Humble yourselves in the sight of the Lord, and he will lift you up" (NKJV).

We were extremely close. We showed the salt to one another—very up close and personal. I loved it that way; being honest and real with each other was like breathing. It was a great comfort during the hard times as we navigated life. I knew in the depths of my heart that God made our mother-daughter relationship extra special. Gosh, I miss her. After a long road in the last years of her life, she has gone home to be with Jesus, her redeemer. "For we know that if our temporary, earthly dwelling is destroyed, we have a building from God, and eternal dwelling in the heavens, not made with hands" (2 Corinthians 5:1 HCSB).

It took me quite some time to not be angry with our gracious God when I had to say those words out loud. Now, I am forever grateful having her heavenly presence flow within my heart and spirit. On this day that the creator has made, she is no longer suffering from an unwavering sadness or what this broken world handed her, and she is made whole. "The Lord is close to the brokenhearted and saves those who are crushed in spirit" (Psalm 34:18 NIV). He is always near the brokenness of life. I have seen it first hand and it was more than a gift.

Servant's Heart

My mother heard her calling from God and obeyed His word to be a servant. It was a true blessing. I reminded her of that blessing when I was trying to cheer her up on the days she felt lost. I could hear the smile in her voice as she would remember all the wonderful memories of her place in this world. Her compassion was immeasurable as a nurse. It could never be documented—only stored away in the heart of God. She truly was a nurturer and cared for others deeply. She could make the hurt and sick laugh or make them feel good by just being herself—funny and at times a little inappropriate! She loved—and I mean loved—all her patients she cared for during her hospice days and taking care of newborns. Many times, as a fifteen-year-old girl, I would say, "Okay, Momma! I have heard this story before!" Naturally, as a teen, it would annoy me to hear her repeat the stories. I am so happy that I know now the immense love she felt by being a part of her patients' sweet journeys.

Showing her heart to so many she had the privilege of caring for during her thirty-five years of nursing filled her spirit from the Lord, and it shined. Ephesians 6:7 says, "Serve wholeheartedly, as if you were serving the Lord, not people" (HCSB). That, she did.

Fondest Childhood Memories

When I was a little girl, she would fill up my cup with:

Waking up to a Valentine's Day card and heart candy, or

little lunch notes that made my heart soar with a sense of belonging.

She coached my first-grade T-ball team, and we were undefeated.

She taught at the preschool I attended so we could be together.

Knowing she was a baby nurse for Dr. Wells filled me with pride because my momma took care of babies. I was overjoyed to be her baby. I felt safe.

She made me behave. She was stern and grace-filled all at once.

She was beautiful inside and out. Both of my girls endure that beauty, too.

Most importantly, her love for Jesus taught me to always run to Him no matter my life circumstances and to trust God to accomplish what I cannot.

He always will do it better. Always. All He asks of you is to use His mighty strength on your troubled days. "Seek the Lord and His strength; seek His presence continually!" (Psalm 105:4).

Moving Day

Once upon a time,
This little girl's life turned on a dime.
She had to move across the big ol' Texas state—
I leaned into my mother's trust and Godly faith.
She knew that she would deeply miss all her sweet playmates.
Starting over for her family was the case.
It soon entailed the real brokenness they had to face.
It was all making her so anxious and nervous.
Because her life suddenly felt like a big circus.
Prayers to Jesus poured from her young heart.
She asked Him to be there from the very start.

Corinne King

The Single Years

After we moved my parents divorced, I was in the fourth grade. Unexpected at the time, their divorce became a deep scar woven into the fabric of our lives. My momma remained strong and steady, though I could tell she was drenched in sadness, completely carrying all the shame. As a kid, I vividly remember her having a family Bible study at home. I felt God there each time, with His guidance and abundance of love. Then and there, she taught my young Godly spirit to lean on Him with any circumstance. She practiced Proverbs 22:6, which says, "Train up a child in the way he should go: and when he is old he will not depart from it" (KJV).

As an adult with a mature Godly spirit, I understand why she carried out the Bible study. It was during the heartbreak of her life and the breaking of her children's foundation that she needed to draw us all closer into God's divine power. She reminded us that, "For ever since the world was created, people have seen the earth and sky. Through everything God made, they can clearly see his invisible qualities, his eternal power and divine nature. So they have no excuse for not knowing God" (Romans 1:20 NIV). She was illustrating her love of God and how to remain faithful when life makes a person feel anything but faithful—a lesson that I have fallen back on countless times in my own life story.

During the sad period that changed our insides forever, her precious actions of playing kid games and constantly laughing with us kept us smiling. It allowed us to see that even though our insides had changed, God is the same forever, just like Hebrews 13:8 says, "Jesus Christ is the same yesterday, today, and forever" (HCSB). For that, I am eternally grateful.

Through her serving spiritual truth to us, along with our childlike faith, we learned that God will literally sit inside you forever, no matter how much it hurts at the time. He will never forsake you. God showered us with joy and love in the small things right there inside our new little apartment. He knew that our bond would grow stronger and deeper in those formative years of my childhood because of the pain we both felt and the unconditional love we had for each other.

Job 8:21 promises, "He will once again fill your mouth with laughter and your lips with shouts of joy" (NLT). We were her joy. I knew she was trying to make it all better with her sweet motherly instincts, and that's all my fourth-grader self needed.

My Dark

The day I woke up in my new beginning
I remember seeing and feeling the yellow sunlight
Coming through the shades so intently, so bright.
It was streaming into my insides that felt so uneasy but so glad.
Glad my life could change from being complicated and sad.
My momma had put her strong-willed daughter in her place.
It was hard for her to drop me off into that much-needed space.
She knew with all her heart I wasn't being who I was truly—
With all my young-adult decisions, I was acting unruly.
Extreme tough love is what she showed me that day.
She came and took me away
From the crazy and unrighteous life I was living.
I needed her comfort and direction that she was giving.
For my enriched and blessed present life,
I will always be forever grateful
That God made her my momma so I could see
She would absolutely never give up on me.

Takes a Turn

My mother was practical and stable in my childhood eyes…until she wasn't in my adulthood years, and it scared me to my core.

Joshua 1:9 says, "Have I not commanded you? Be strong and courageous. Do not be afraid; do not be discouraged, for the Lord your God will be with you, wherever you go" (NIV). I clung to this belief—and God's promise and command—as I observed my momma at her lowest of lows. In August of 2021, she caught covid and had to be hospitalized with no visits allowed. God willing, she survived. I prayed so intently that God would not take her and He knew that she did not want to die alone. She needed her kids to be with her when she went to heaven. Before she had covid, I witnessed her almost pass away on several occasions from her kidney disease and having a stroke. She never fully recovered from her first stroke. I was devastated and extremely hurt seeing my momma so unhappy. Her emotional state of reality became weaker and weaker. I was her reality, and both Minden and Mary were her reality. It was hard for my heart to understand. "Trust in the Lord with all your heart, and do not rely on your own understanding; think about Him in all your ways, and He will guide you on the right paths" (Proverbs 3:5–6 HCSB). Making her feel and be whole again was a mission that I pursued with all my might. I prayed for her without ceasing, like Thessalonians 5:16–18 directs, "Rejoice always, pray without ceasing, give thanks in all circumstances; for this is the will of God in Christ Jesus for you" (ESV).

I cried out to God from the depths of my heart for guidance, as I knew only He understood the severity of how truly complicated my momma's condition was. Exodus 14:14 says, "The Lord will fight for you while you [only need to] keep silent and remain calm" (AMP). Remembering my momma's words from her Bible study long ago, I was reminded that He already won the battle and fights for His children, and it gave me peace beyond measure. I clung to Jesus just as she did, to His promises and His love in the dark times, and I was deeply grateful to Him that I could. Jesus and I understood each other because of my momma.

I desperately wanted my mother to be whole again and for God to return her back to me. Through the midst of my wants, Jesus became my greatest teacher and taught me only He could make her whole again and "fix" her life. She was still there, just in a different way. Her mind and body might have been different, but her heart would never change. So, I had to make a decision to trust God and not to be bitter about the pain of my momma becoming sick and changing. I had to let go and be happy with my blessed life, for which I worked so hard through my own trying times. I know my momma cried out deep in her heart for me to do that very thing—to let go of what I couldn't control and to stop worrying about her all the time. See, she was still the same—always wanting the best for me—and she never once quit being my mother.

I feared losing her to the life choices she had made after she got sick and tired of being sick and tired. So, naturally, I was angry and controlling. I was mean and domineering. We were not good on so many days. I just kept praying for God to soften my heart and open my eyes on how to love her where she stood. She deserved that as a person, and she really deserved that from our deep and personal God-given mother-daughter relationship. And guess what, she absolutely knew her eldest daughter would react in this manner toward her not-so-good choices. She raised me and always said, "I know you like the back of my hand." Still to this day her words give my heart so much comfort. Because she did know me and always will.

The day we had to move her from the assisted living facility to the nursing home broke my heart. It was extremely hard knowing this was the last option for her living situation. I was so afraid because I knew this was it for her life as I knew it. She was scared, too, and that broke my heart even more. My oldest childhood best friend came to hold my hand through it all and helped me to focus on the hope. This friend and my mother loved each other deeply. They had very similar upbringings and stood on common ground spiritually—still do and always will. She eased my worry and the pain I had gone through all my life because of the history of my parents. Love you, best friend, and I'm eternally grateful you are mine. You and I are both stronger than we know because Jesus is our refuge. "The Lord is a shelter for the oppressed. A refuge in times of trouble" (Psalm 9:9).

Grandma loved yellow roses.
They will eventually take a turn too.
But will always remain beautiful like just her.

Corinne King

Simply Beautiful

By this time in our lives, I became a mother, and we loved to feed the ducks at the park when we visited Grandma. It became a simple and sweet activity that we could all enjoy together. Even though my mother was bound to her wheelchair, this outing would get her out in nature, and she could watch her grandbabies run around together. One afternoon, after our visit with the ducks, we headed over to the local coffee shop and enjoyed the sunshine. Mary was about 8 months old. That was when I realized that my momma's mind was truly diminishing. She sweetly looked at her baby granddaughter, and said, "Corinne, she is beautiful." It was almost like she was in another reality and meeting her for the very first time. My heart sank. I knew we were losing her and she would never be the same. I can always hear her sweet voice saying, "Corinne, she is beautiful." She was so proud and happy that it made my heart feel unbelievably thankful for that sweet visit, getting to see her in that moment with her granddaughter, as they were fleeting. It was simply beautiful.

Corinne King

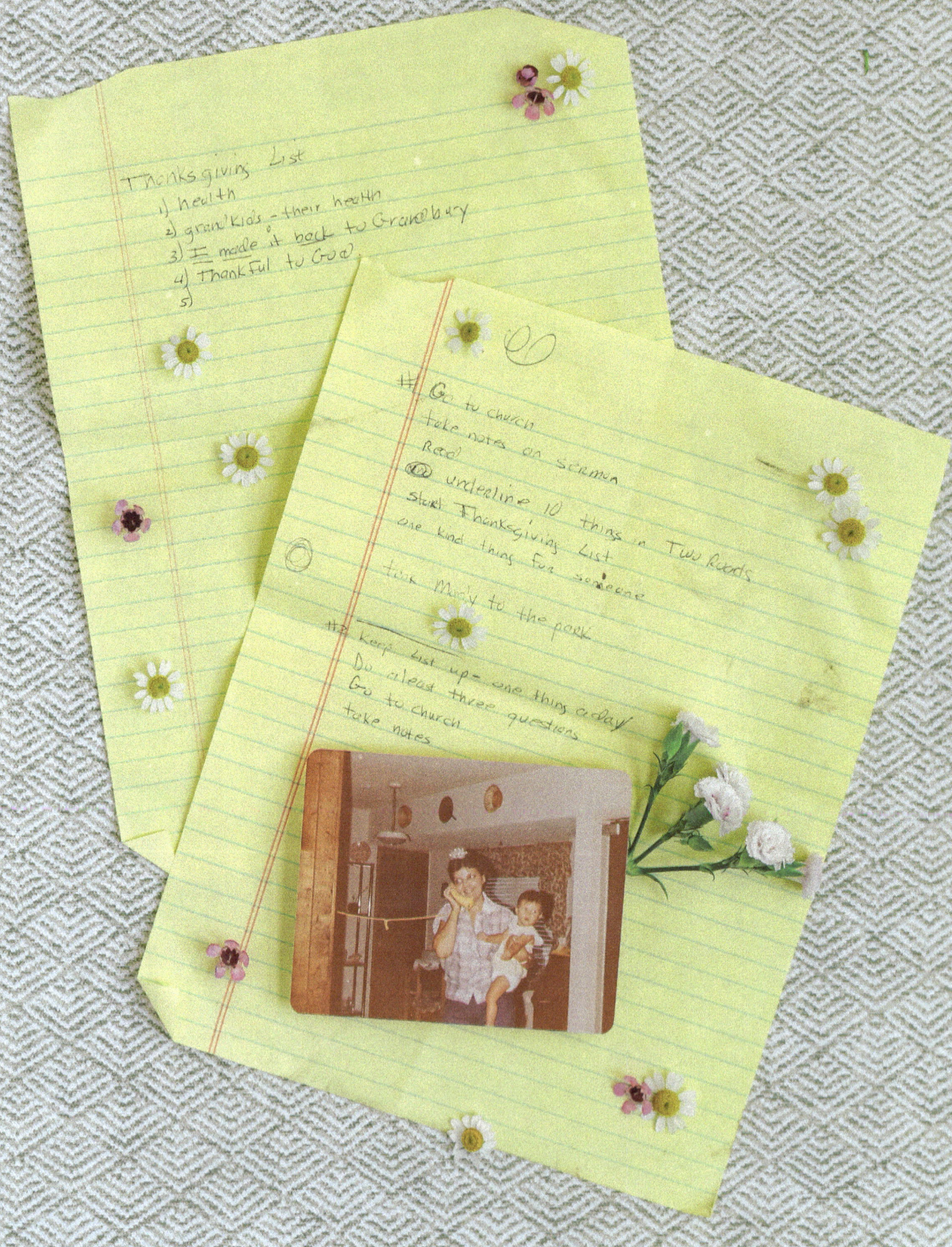

Answered Prayers

As my momma's health was declining and her depression grew right in front of my weepy eyes, again I became controlling and angry. She was making poor life choices by not taking care of her mental or physical health, and my fear of the unknown was developing rapidly and deeply. All the heavy emotions were getting the best of me. I prayed and prayed for God to calm my rocky waters. Thankfully, God counseled my heart to control my hasty temper and not behave like a fool. He reminded me of Ecclesiastes 7:9, "Don't be too quick to get angry because anger lives in the fool's heart" (CEB). And my momma didn't raise no fool!

One of God's amazing gifts is that He cares about every detail and carries the control, for all of us. He gave me such a gift in life, even though my mother was slowly losing hers. He could have brought her home to heaven many times during her decade-long health battle. All the while I was still choosing to be angry, controlling, and miserable with her. His will chose not to and showed us both grace.

In Psalm 31:15, He reminds us, "My times are in Your hands" (NIV). In His perfect time, He knew when she would be free in heaven. Not a moment too soon and not a moment too late. So that our hearts could return to the peace, love, and truth that we both deserved. And the truth was we loved each other beyond measure, without a doubt. He wanted to remind us both of that before she passed. A few short months before she went home, God gave my uneasy soul such a profound blessing. He gave me peace with where she ended up in life and the realization I had to get control over my emotions. This wasn't about me. I reminded myself that this was between her and God, and He loved her more. She was ready to go home where she knew she could truly let go.

Another beautiful piece to the puzzle, and a big answered prayer that my heart desperately needed to witness, was her receiving peace before she passed. She felt my peace toward her with love, and that did it for her—peace. The majority of my life, she was excellent at faking a smile for her children, but inside she was deeply hurt. I knew she was beyond ready to be free with Jesus and not feel broken anymore. But she knew she couldn't leave this world yet. If I was not in the best place emotionally or spiritually with her, she wouldn't be able to let go. She needed to feel in her soul and see with her own eyes that I was okay with her life choices and happy in my own life. Now, this is my hope and daily prayer—sometimes every minute—to remember her God-given goodness. The true love that she had for her children was the essence of who she truly was as a person—not her broken outward appearance or existence. She needed me to live out all her wonderful parts and carry out the deep connection we both shared because it was made from the love of God. "We love because he first loved us" (1 John 4:19 NIV). Our deep love that we had for each other is for me to pass to you, her legacy and her granddaughters.

God is the love that flows from our hearts. Nothing else matters to Him. And when we love others like He does, we show Him how much we love and adore Him.

God didn't remove the Red Sea. He parted it. God doesn't always remove your problems, but He will make a way to get through them.

The Awaiting Day

My momma passed away in peace with me, my sister, and my brother by her side. I was the last one to arrive. I could just imagine my mother saying, "Where is she? I am ready to go on!" She waited for me. She always has, and this would be the last time. I was there for around thirteen minutes when the hospice nurse drew us near and told us it was her time.

A dear friend from the Bible study I led had sent a message to me that very morning. I knew God had sent it, from her prayers for us. I leaned over her hospice bed and read the message to her sweet face, *"God didn't remove the Red Sea. He parted it. God doesn't always remove your problems, but He will make a way to get through them."*

She was gone moments later. It was breathtaking to see her go be with the King of Kings, the Promise Keeper, the Redeemer, and Yahweh. As Isaiah righteously says, "Fear not, for I am with you; be not dismayed, for I am your God; I will strengthen you, I will help you, I will uphold you with my righteous right hand." She was now holding His hand. It was real.

Friendly Love

I had an epiphany on the long twilight drive back to my house that afternoon.

I had no words for Jesus.

It was such a foreign feeling to my spirit it rattled me. I had been in such deep and intense prayer related to my mother for so long. I had stayed in constant communication with God about her, our relationship, and our family for almost a decade. Just a few weeks earlier, I had been praying for Him to take her home to be free from this world. I was always praying for God to do His best for her, just as she always did for me.
1 Thessalonians 5:17 tells us to pray without ceasing. I obeyed and was always in prayer for my momma's peace and relief from pain, both physically and mentally.

Suddenly, **I no longer needed to pray** about it and didn't know what to say to Him. She was literally sitting with Him now, and she no longer needed my prayers that only He understood. It was hard for me to grasp that reality. I was stunned that I felt so distant from His being. I didn't expect that part at all.

I was explaining this realization to one of my sweetest God-fearing friends the next day. Her exact words went straight to my soul when she said, "Friend, you better get ready, because it's coming, and He is going to need you to pray again like you did for your momma!" Her words meant everything to me at that perfect moment and spoke His truth into my pain. "Oil and incense bring joy to the heart, and the pleasantness of a friend springs from their heartfelt advice" (Proverbs 27:9 NIV). Thank you, friend, for being the oil and incense to my heart when it needed to find God's joy again.

Corinne King

Angry With God

I want to be the one to tell my girls that it is quite all right to be angry with God. He understands that we live in a broken world and knows that our faith will alter because of our sufferings. He created our souls to long for His divine sovereignty during our pain. So go ahead and be mad. He is a big boy and can handle our big-girl emotions. He created them, and we can never hide from Him. "We glory in our sufferings, because we know that suffering produces perseverance; perseverance, character, and character, hope" (Romans 5:3–4 NIV). I put this verse on a yellow sticky note on my bathroom vanity to see every morning and to be reminded that I will always have hope, because of Jesus.

My soul felt so lost after my momma passed away, and still does on occasion. I now understand this part of grief. I was so angry with God that I had to deal with the grief of losing her, in my mind, for such a senseless reason. In my mind she gave up and she knew I felt that way. When I walked into the hospital room after her second stroke, I climbed into her bed—as we both knew she would never recover and was about to go home to Jesus. I hugged her and gave her a kiss on the cheek. She said to me, "I am so sorry that I didn't take better care of myself for you."
I told her, "Momma, please don't worry about that anymore and just be in Jesus's peace." It was her time to go. God was with us both, just like He always had been. That was such a precious and peaceful moment that I get to hold on to forever. She knew that my heart needed to hear those words. She was sorry. I was, too.

She passed three weeks after her massive stroke. Shortly after, the disconnect between God and me because of her death was making me angry with Him. So, one day I let Him have it, and I know He just smiled, nodded, and said, "Oh, there she is." He was waiting for me to come to Him with all I was thinking, feeling, and doing while trying to push down my anger, grief, and insecurity about how and where she died. For my human heart, the story of my mother and me should not be over.

The feeling of insecurity rushed over me, and it was such a foreign way of living. I was going mad, full of anxiety for allowing myself to feel this way because I had never felt this insecurity in my life. I had always felt so incredibly confident and secure because of who I was in Him. Now that had changed. I was angry and scared. On repeat, I would visualize leaving these heavy burdens at the **foot of the cross**. They weren't mine to carry. I knew this, as Matthew 11:28 (NIV) says, "Come to me, all you who are weary and burdened, and I will give you rest." Over time, His truth returned to my weary soul, and the anxiety of what I felt started to lift away. He knew this would happen in my faith, and He used this burden to refine me, to draw me closer into His peace. Once again, God works in mysterious ways. I just adore Him and love all the beauty He possesses.

Through my grief and suffering, He was refining me to understand that my mother didn't pass away for a senseless reason—absolutely nothing is senseless when you belong to Him and His will. I still had Him, even though I was angry about losing my wonderful mother. "The Lord himself goes before you and will be with you; he will never leave you nor forsake you. Do not be afraid; do not be discouraged" (Joshua 31:8 NLT). I see this verse clearer more than ever now because of my great loss. I grew to be grateful, knowing that my pain was not in vain. He was there with me even when my heart felt distant.

Shine On

Starting to Heal

I can feel the wholeness of God's truth starting to patch up my heart. Patchwork done by God repeatedly is the best sort of work, and I have experienced a lot of it.

"We know that all things work together for the good of those who love God: those who are called according to His purpose" (Romans 8:28 HCSB). Jesus's earthly suffering was part of His purpose so we could be redeemed and have His peace. That is what it is all about, right there. His purpose was to save us, because He loves us more than we could ever know and He wants a personal relationship. The great suffering He endured was the last and final sacrifice, so we could never really die. We get to spend eternal life with Him forever. Makes me beam with happiness.

During my despair of mourning and fear, I knew deep down that God would bless me with His riches once again. "Blessed are the poor in spirit: for theirs is the kingdom of heaven. Blessed are they that mourn: for they shall be comforted" (Matthew 5:3–4 KJV).

He kept whispering to me in all the soft places, "Surrender to me, and look up to the paradise where your momma's gypsy soul is living and dwell in the heavenly ways. A big piece of your heart lives here now." That is the truth of the matter. "In the beginning God created the heavens and the earth" (Genesis 1:1 KJV). In His mighty hands, both heaven and earth lie together. She is still here, and I am there.

Losing her, and especially the outcome of her story, utterly shocked my entire being—spirit, soul, mind, and heart. It stunned me that I could no longer talk her ear off and have her attentively listen to my every word. Over time, God showed that frazzled heart of mine the truth, that I had a momma who would listen and I should be thankful for that blessing. She made it clear my entire life she valued the joy and love that I gave the world from inside my soul; now she is enjoying it from heaven.

The spiritual truth she taught me and I believed all my life slowly started to fill my cup up once again. This earth is not our home; we are just passing through.

My precious momma is now with our Lord and Savior. As hard as it is not to see her and have her voice to calm my mind and heart, I must rejoice that she is beyond the pearly gates of heaven! Rejoice, rejoice! His faithful servant is home.

A Mother's Gift

On the night of my forty-third birthday, I laid down to have bedtime chats with my Minden girl. I was really missing my momma's sweet voice wishing me a happy birthday. I could feel her peace in the room as Minden's big blue eyes looked up at me and she said, "I love our small talk." My heart swelled with pride and joy that I had never felt before. Our deep connected love took my breath away, as I knew this was why I loved my momma so much. Right then and there, I knew what it was all about...this emotional ride called motherhood.

In that exact moment, all my daughter needed in the whole entire world was for me to intently listen to her important words, just as my momma would listen to mine. My momma knew just by listening to me it would complete my tiny little world, just like I completed my daugther's tiny little world at that exact moment. It was my turn, and I had learned from the best. My momma's spirit was still with us in that sweet birthday moment, showing me the importance of motherhood. A good mother's role in their children's lives is to believe in them with all her heart. So when they are sent out into the world they will shine—perhaps through the love you selflessly served one night when they were nine years old, just by listening.

The next day, I woke up with a peace in my spirit I hadn't felt in quite some time. It felt like an old friend was calling just to say "hello." More each day, I feel her presence from heaven and less of the despair that I had completely lost her forever. As believers, we understand the doctrine that Jesus died to forgive us for our sins and that we will have an everlasting life in heaven with Him. I felt so lost and wavering the day my heart knew she was gone. I was scared, but also comforted by the truth that Jesus knew this particular season would test my faith. "I am the Alpha and the Omega, the First and the Last, the Beginning and the End" (Revelation 22:13 NIV). He is sovereign over it all, find rest in that promise.

My heart and head are finally aligning with the reality that she is not completely gone. I had sensed this was her birthday present from heaven, for me to truly realize her spirit lives within me and her precious granddaughters, forever.

Letters

A collection of letters from the heart for my dear mother,
mother-in-law, and especially for my two precious daughters.

Shine On

Corinne King

Dear Minden Grace and Mary Lafitte,

I never met your great grandmother, Mary Johnson. She went to heaven before I was born just like your grandmother, Marylin Johnson. The three of us have in common that we have never met one of our grandmothers. I feel it in my bones that God has something to do with this part of our story that connects us. It's a God-wink, I'd say!

Both "MJ"'s were strong, southern, God-fearing women. I will never understand, nor am I supposed to understand, the reason they were not a part of our life's journey. I ponder on the reality that my sweet momma didn't have her own mother to help when she was raising her babies. I now understand how difficult that must have been for her when she needed reassurance in motherhood the most—especially when she went through her divorce and one of her darkest times. Her mother's absence taught her to lean into God's hope and truth, too. God works in mysterious ways to teach His children to surrender it all to Him.

Truly, I feel the comfort that you both have locked eyes with your Grandma Sheila and that she was able to hold your sweet little hand, unlike me with my grandmother MJ and you with your grandmother MJ.

Not having my grandmother around had to be painful and sad to work through alone. Grandma was strong and took motherhood by the horns on her own, and for that I will be forever grateful. I can only imagine how she ran so fast into her mother's arms. It was a tight hug bursting with joy and comfort when she walked into the Kingdom of Heaven! On the last days of being with your grandma, she spoke to me about how she could see her mom and they were speaking to each other in the heavenly realms. I smiled, and I knew she was ready for the peace that was coming her way. She needed rest and to see her momma. Rest assured, sweet girls, you have the best guardian angels watching over you. They love you beyond and will always root for you from heaven!

Love always,

Momma

Dear Marilyn,

I am sitting here in my office working on my book, with God, for your beautiful granddaughters, and your very own Richard walked in to bring me lunch. So, I am now enjoying my favorite **french fries** from one of our favorite lunch spots in town, Local Foods. Perfectly sprinkled with salt, pepper, and a little chili powder. Simply the best, just like him. With that, I want to like to say thank you for being a big part of the reason he is filled with love and commitment, and has a sound mind and a big heart. Most importantly, he was blessed with your good sense of humor. He keeps our household laughing, especially when our girl emotions are running high! God knew we needed him, and I pray daily for him to know what to do with us, as we are strong ones! I know you aren't surprised and love that fact!

I recently found a prayer list I wrote in 1993. My #5 prayer was:

Charli and I have good husbands, and we're good wives. We have a good education, kids, money, and jobs. And Russell has a good wife, and he is a good husband, and has an education, job, money, and kids.

Obviously, I loved my brother, sister, and momma. But I had no idea how much I could love your son. We have been through a lot of life's hardships together and hold on to each other's strength tightly. You were sadly faced with the unknown of not being a part of your children's future. I can't imagine how devastating that feeling must have been for your wishes and dreams as a mother. I can feel within me that you prayed deeply for your dear son's wife to be

God-loving and -fearing. I want you to know from the bottom of my heart that I strive and pray to be that wife you prayed for many years ago. I know you feel them in heaven, too, and that you are with my momma. I can just hear both of you talking about Richard and **Corinne** and how funny we are with each other. You both get to leap in the joy of knowing that both your prayers were answered, for your Richard and for her **Corinne**. Your granddaughters are thriving and loving their blessed lives because of your great legacy. They are amazing and thoughtful humans, just like you.

I am forever grateful that you raised a man who loves the Lord and his three girls with all his might. He spreads love so well because of the love you gave him. So, thank you, Grandma Marilyn. I enjoy being his wife and am so very blessed that my thirteen-year-old prayer was answered through your boy, Richard.

Love,

your daughter-in-law, Corinne

Corinne King

Dear Minden and Mary,

I miss her. I miss her desperately when I need her reassurance in motherhood. I need to hear her voice to quiet my own voice telling me, *You really messed up their hearts this time!* I need her to rescue me from my shameful mistakes and put a big red bow on it. But truthfully, God can only quiet that voice and redeem the shameful feelings of making mistakes in motherhood. I have read the closest comparison to God's love is the love of a mother for her child. I am incredibly blessed that I get to experience that bondage of love between us. My love for you two beautiful souls runs so deep in my existence. It brings me an abundance of joy. I love you both through and through in this broken world. God doesn't operate out of our broken and sinful world like we do. He designed it that way so He can love us more and work all things out for our good! I am just in awe of Him.

I have always asked you both since you could speak, "Who loves you more than Mommy and Daddy?" You would grin big and say without hesitation, "Jesus!" I pray that you always keep the childlike faith. It makes God grin, too, because it is true, my darlings—he does love you more than I could ever be capable of loving you. As life was designed to flow, and my momma has gone on to receive the great reward in heaven she so rightfully deserves, the story becomes ours to live, my sweet girls. In Grandma's last days on this earth she would constantly tell me to pray over everything. Just pray. I love that I can remember her sweet voice saying, "just pray." The greatest advice a mother could ever say to her daughter and now she is passing that down to both of you. Just pray. God hears you. She promises.

xoxoxo,

Momma

Dear Momma,

The pain I feel from losing you is so raw and real that sometimes it physically hurts my insides. It is unreal to me. How can I let the pain of not having you here for my girls consume me? One day, I decided to sit and ponder and let the pain wash over me so it would pass. This, too, shall pass. But something this big? Really? Never in a million years did I think I would not have you around to be part of my children's lives. My heart cries at the fact you would have been the most dreamy grandma with your sweet touch and loving hugs.

On the other side of the pain, I know with all my heart the *big* love you have for us is bigger than the burden of losing you slowly the way we did. Psalm 55:22 tells us, "Cast your burden on the Lord and He will sustain you" (HCSB). You absolutely would not want to be a burden to me because of your choices, or for me to carry that pain around in my heart. We're told in Proverbs 4:23, "Above all else, guard your heart, for everything you do flows from it" (NIV). This is not our story. It is God's story. This is why I love you so much. The pain ran deep because the love was so deep. I have learned to live with both as Jesus did. He is my teacher. In this world, I must live in the joy of love and the pain of suffering. That is where I find His gift of peace—the true peace.

My deepest sorrow is needing to forgive you for not taking care of yourself like you deserved. I am forgiving you for myself, your beautiful granddaughters, and for my beautiful marriage—quintessentially, for my people. **"Be kind to one another, tenderhearted, forgiving one another, as God in Christ forgave you" Ephesians 4:32 (ESV).** I am forgiving you, as God has forgiven me, too. I don't want to harbor bitterness and resentment in my heart. I know both you and God are smiling down from heaven cheering me on, so I can continue my race before me in peace, love, and joy just like you prayed for.

I hope that our love story teaches Minden and Mary to pray for the Lord to help them forgive those they love, as well as for those who love them, when it hurts. God's Word tells us in Mark 11:25, "And wherever you stand praying, forgive, if you have anything against anyone, so that your Father also who is in heaven may forgive you your trespasses" (ESV). Thank you, Momma, for showing me that our gracious Lord created forgiveness in this broken world to protect His children from sin so that we find His peace. His perfect design is truly out of this world, and I am forever grateful that I have found His peace because of you.

Love you with all my heart. See you in heaven.

xoxoxo,

Mary Corinne

In Conclusion

Dear Lord in Heaven,

I pray that by sharing the sweet and hard journey that my momma and I had before she went to heaven will help other daughters and mothers to see that your joy can always be found. All they have to do is to look up. Lord help guide their hearts closer to you and to give thanks for their whole relationship forever, no matter their worldly circumstances. Thank you, Lord, for their laughter and the love they share. And always, thank you so much for giving me such a great momma. I wouldn't be where I am today without her true love. Thank you for it all.

In Jesus' precious name I pray, Amen.

About the Author

Corinne King lives in Fort Worth, Texas with her husband, two daughters and two little brown dogs. Her heart beats for community service, where she enthusiastically volunteers with multiple charitable organizations. She loves to share food, wine and Jesus with everyone around her while laughing and bringing spice to life.

About the Photographer

Analisa Brewer is a photographer residing in Fort Worth, TX with her wonderful husband and two precious kiddos who keep her super busy and bring so much joy to life! In addition to her passion for photography and love for spending time with her family, she enjoys an acoustic version of almost any song, fitness of all kinds, dancing, spending time with Jesus, and a good heart-to-heart over a cup of coffee.

www.ingramcontent.com/pod-product-compliance
Lightning Source LLC
Chambersburg PA
CBHW061353010526
44107CB00011B/923